INTERFACT LADDERS

Wild Animals

TWO CAN

LONDON ▪ PRINCETON

www.two-canpublishing.com

Published by Two-Can Publishing
43-45 Dorset Street, London W1U 7NA

www.two-canpublishing.com

© Two-Can Publishing 2002

For information on Two-Can books and multimedia,
call (0)20 7224 2440, fax (0)20 7224 7005
or visit our website at http://www.two-canpublishing.com

Created by
act-two
346 Old Street
London EC1V 9RB

www.act-two.com

Written by: Sarah Fecher and Deborah Kespert
Edited by: Lisa Miles
Story by: Belinda Webster
Consultants: Dr. Iram Siraj-Blatchford, Institute of Education, London;
Sandi Bain, London Zoo; Sandra Jenkins
Art director: Belinda Webster
Design: Amanda McCourt and Liz Adcock
Main illustrations: Peter Utton
Computer illustrations: Jon Stuart
Line illustrations: Andy Hamilton

'Two-Can' is a trademark of Two-Can Publishing.
Two-Can Publishing is a division of Zenith Entertainment plc,
43-45 Dorset Street, London W1U 7NA

1-84301-037-2

Dewey Decimal Classification 599

10 9 8 7 6 5 4 3 2 1

A catalogue record for this book is available from the British Library.

Photographic credits: p6: Zefa; p8: Ardea Ltd; p9: Tony Stone Images; p10: Ardea Ltd;
p12: Ardea Ltd; p13: Tony Stone Images; p14: Tony Stone Images; p15: Planet Earth Pictures;
p18: Oxford Scientific Films; p21: Planet Earth Pictures; p22: BBC Natural History Unit;
p24: BBC Natural History Unit; p25: Natural History Photographic Agency.

Printed in Hong Kong by Wing King Tong

What's inside?

All of the wild animals in this book live in Africa. They make their homes on dry land covered with grass, which stretches as far as your eyes can see.

What's on the disk?

There are great games to play on the disk. Drive through the African grasslands in your jeep and visit the animals. Each one takes you to an exciting game. Look out for the big elephant. It leads you to an extra surprise!

▶ Here's the screen that takes you to your games. Just drive up and visit each animal!

snapshots

chimpanzee

ostrich

lion

hippo

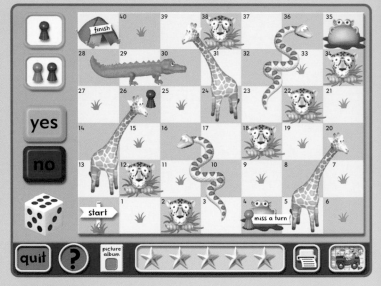

picture album
Your picture album
When you play a game, you win an animal photo for your picture album. There are four photos to collect altogether. Just click on each one to see the animal in action!

DISK LINK
Race to safety!
Visit the ostrich to play snakes and ladders in the grasslands. As you race to the camp, there are questions to answer, mud pools to jump and dangerous animals to dodge!

DISK LINK

At the waterhole
Visit the hippo and see if you can spot the animals at the waterhole. Watch what happens when you get your answers right!

DISK LINK

Animal spotter
Visit the lion to play this animal markings game. Grab your spotter's notebook, then match each animal to its coat.

DISK LINK

Jigsaw fun!
Visit the chimpanzee to make two fantastic animal jigsaws. To play, match each word to its picture, then drag the pieces into place. There's a printout prize to colour in too!

DISK LINK

It's a bonus!
After finishing two games, catch up with the elephant to play a bonus game. Guess each animal in the magnifying glass and win stickers to make a super safari scene.

Rhinoceros

A rhinoceros, or rhino for short, lives by itself. It spends the day dozing on the grass, nibbling at plants and rolling around in wet mud to cool down. All the other animals keep out of its way because it looks so fierce!

A rhino pulls twigs from a bush with its specially long top lip. It chews the twigs with its flat back teeth.

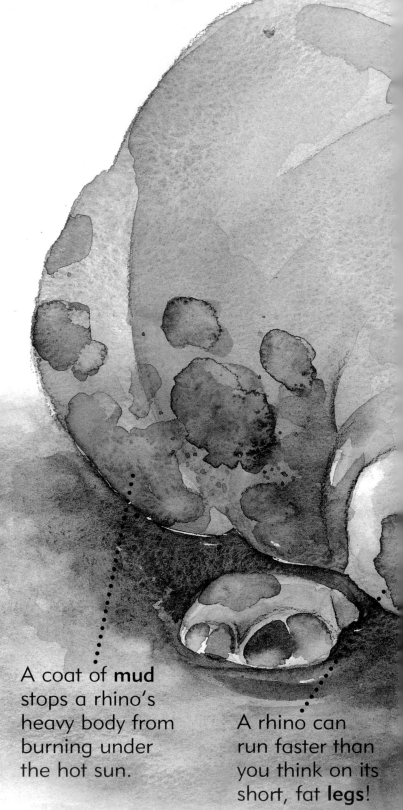

A coat of **mud** stops a rhino's heavy body from burning under the hot sun.

A rhino can run faster than you think on its short, fat **legs**!

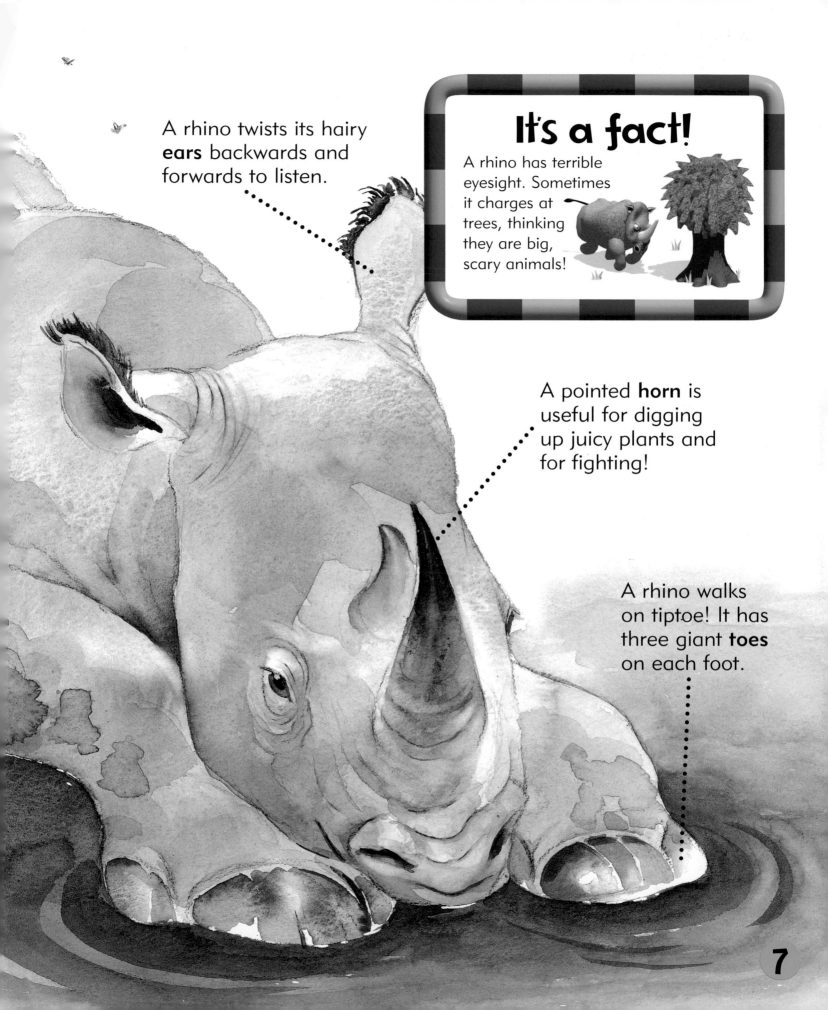

A rhino twists its hairy **ears** backwards and forwards to listen.

It's a fact!

A rhino has terrible eyesight. Sometimes it charges at trees, thinking they are big, scary animals!

A pointed **horn** is useful for digging up juicy plants and for fighting!

A rhino walks on tiptoe! It has three giant **toes** on each foot.

Giraffe

Small groups of giraffes run across the grasslands on their long, slender legs. They are the tallest animals in the world. Giraffes aren't afraid of many animals, but they have to keep an eye out for hungry lions.

A giraffe pulls leaves from the trees with its thick, black **tongue**.

A giraffe stretches its **neck** to reach leaves high up in the trees.

Patchwork **markings** help to hide a giraffe against the trees.

A giraffe bends down a long way to drink. It spreads its front legs wide apart and carefully lowers its head.

It's a fact!

A giraffe can wrap its extremely long tongue right round its head. It even uses it to wash behind its ears!

Two bony **horns** grow from the top of a giraffe's head.

A baby giraffe takes shelter between its mother's legs. Here, it feels snug and safe from enemies.

Thick **eyelashes** protect a giraffe's eyes from wind and dust.

Even the sharpest thorns do not hurt a giraffe's thick **lips** as it eats.

9

# Hippopotamus

Hippopotamuses, or hippos for short, love to spend their days lazing around in muddy water. Here, they keep cool, away from the hot sun. At night, they climb on to the land to munch grass at the water's edge.

Wallowing in the water stops a hippo's thin **skin** from drying out.

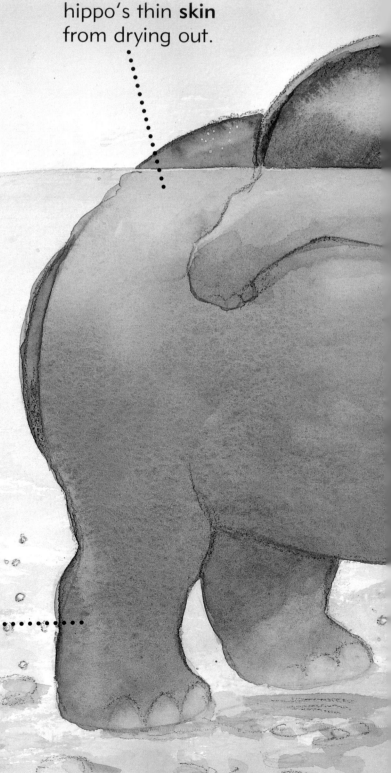

When a hippo is angry, it opens its big mouth as wide as it can and flashes its long, sharp teeth!

A hippo is an excellent swimmer but it also enjoys **walking** along the bottom of the river.

DISK LINK

Visit the hippo to find out about the animals at the waterhole!

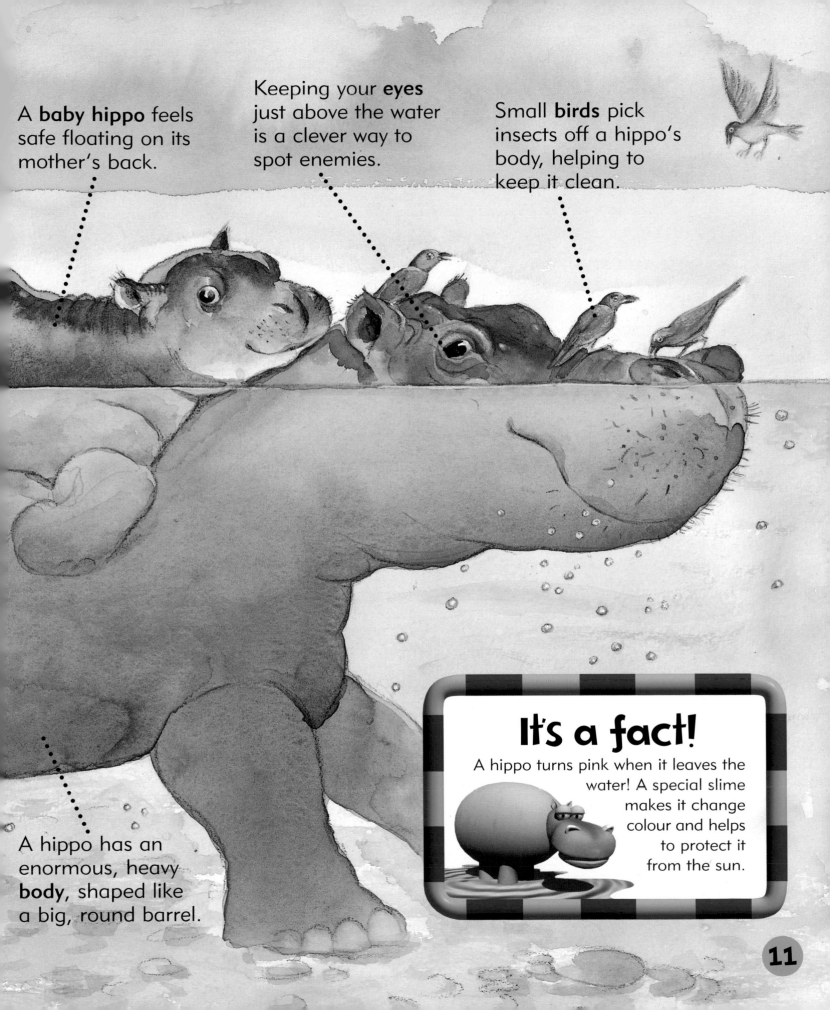

A **baby hippo** feels safe floating on its mother's back.

Keeping your **eyes** just above the water is a clever way to spot enemies.

Small **birds** pick insects off a hippo's body, helping to keep it clean.

A hippo has an enormous, heavy **body**, shaped like a big, round barrel.

It's a fact!

A hippo turns pink when it leaves the water! A special slime makes it change colour and helps to protect it from the sun.

Zebra

Zebras are quiet animals that gather in groups. They wander around, looking for juicy grass to eat. Zebras are afraid of fierce lions. When they spot a hungry lion, they gallop off as fast as they can!

One zebra **listens** for danger while the others nibble at the grass.

A baby zebra stands up soon after it is born. At first, it wobbles on its long legs but it quickly learns how to walk.

A zebra brushes buzzing flies away with its long **tail**.

A bony **hoof** covers each foot and protects it like a shoe.

Look closely and you'll see that the black and white **stripes** on each zebra are different!

Groups of zebras often walk for hours across the dry, hot grasslands to drink from a pool of cool water.

Thick tufts of **hair** stick up from a zebra's neck.

Big, flat **teeth** are good for chewing tough clumps of grass.

 # Lion

Powerful lions live together in groups called prides. Mother lions prowl through the grass, hunting for food. At home, a strong father lion keeps guard. When dinner arrives, the father lion always tucks in first!

A sleepy father lion finds a shady spot in a tree. He dozes here all day long, away from the hot sun.

A shaggy **mane** makes a father lion look big and frightening!

Thick, golden **fur** hides a lion against the dry, yellow grass.

DISK LINK

Visit the lion to match the animals to their coats!

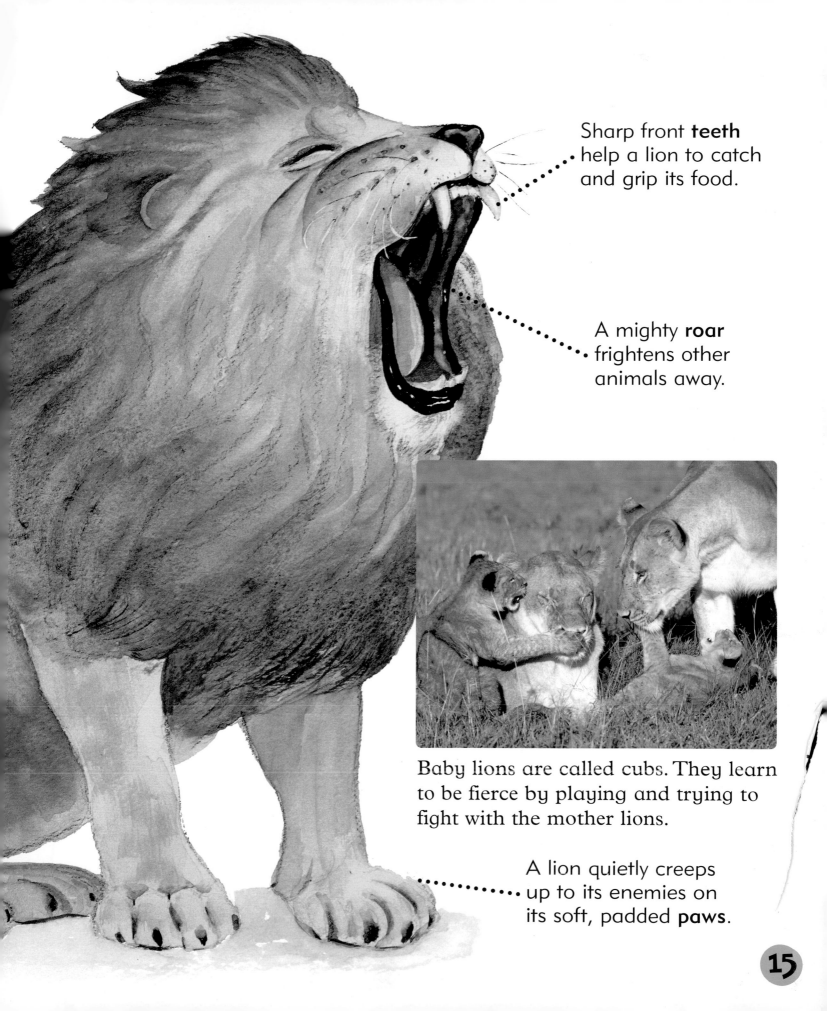

Sharp front **teeth** help a lion to catch and grip its food.

A mighty **roar** frightens other animals away.

Baby lions are called cubs. They learn to be fierce by playing and trying to fight with the mother lions.

A lion quietly creeps up to its enemies on its soft, padded **paws**.

By the water

It's busy by the water this morning! Many animals have travelled a long way to take a cool drink.

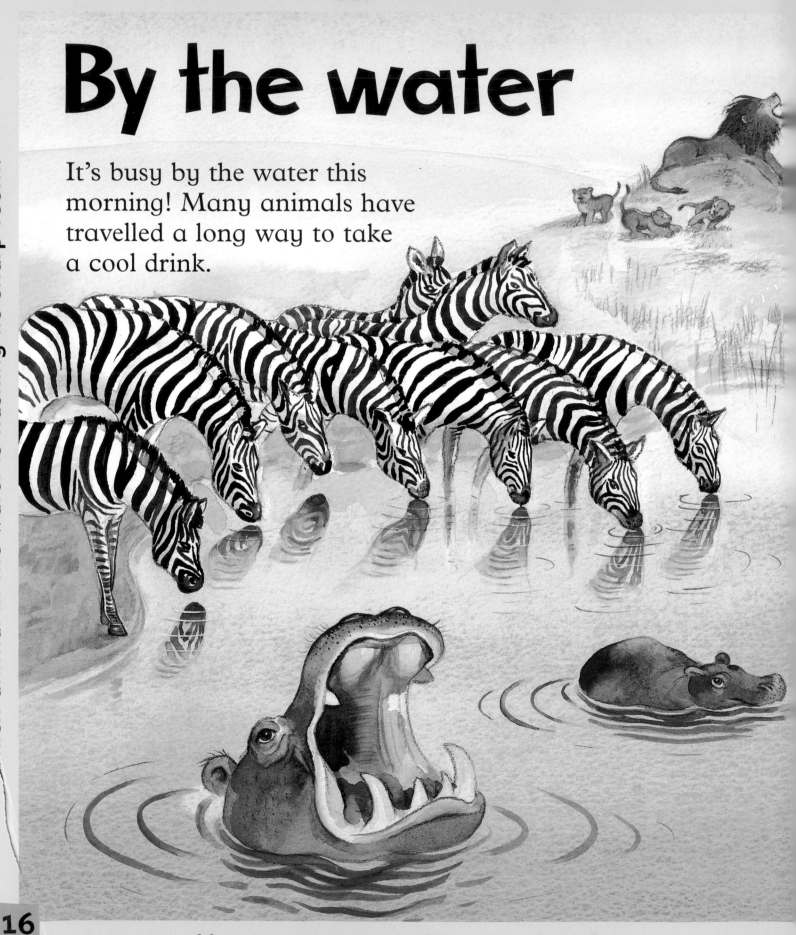

16

What is the hungry giraffe eating?

Words you know

Here are some words that you learned earlier. Say them out loud, then try to find the things in the picture.

hoof	tongue	mane
stripes	lion cub	horn

How does the heavy rhinoceros keep cool?

Elephant

An elephant is the largest animal on land – it has the longest nose in the world, too! An elephant uses its nose, called a trunk, for drinking water, carrying food and making a loud, hooting noise just like a trumpet!

A bendy **trunk** is useful for pulling tasty twigs off trees.

Elephants live in large groups, called herds. They travel a long way across the land looking for food and water.

An elephant sniffs its food through two **nostrils** to tell if it is good to eat.

DISK LINK

Catch up with the elephant to see all kinds of animals close up!

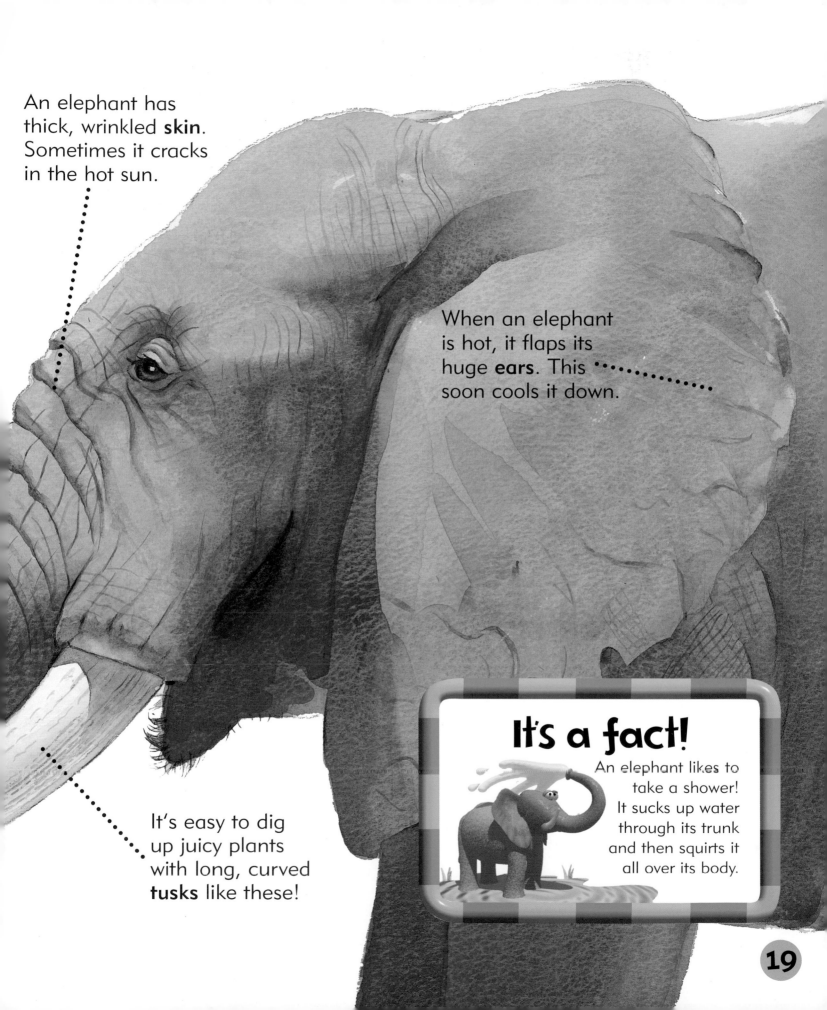

An elephant has thick, wrinkled **skin**. Sometimes it cracks in the hot sun.

When an elephant is hot, it flaps its huge **ears**. This soon cools it down.

It's easy to dig up juicy plants with long, curved **tusks** like these!

It's a fact!

An elephant likes to take a shower! It sucks up water through its trunk and then squirts it all over its body.

Cheetah

During the day, a sneaky cheetah hunts for its dinner. It spots an animal from far away and follows it silently through the grass. Then the cheetah leaps out and chases it as fast as it can. In seconds, the cheetah has a tasty snack to eat!

When a cheetah turns, it holds out its **tail**. This keeps it steady.

A yellow coat with black **spots** hides a cheetah as it moves through the grass.

It's a fact!

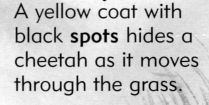

A cheetah runs quicker than any other animal on land. It speeds along as fast as a car on a motorway!

Powerful, long **legs** are best for running quickly.

Many animals are afraid of this sharp **bite**!

Strong **claws** dig into the hard ground and push a cheetah along.

A mother cheetah looks after her silver-haired baby for many months, teaching it how to live in the wild.

21

 # Chimpanzee

Chimpanzees, or chimps for short, live in noisy groups. They look after one another and search for food together. When they're excited, they jump up and down and scream as loudly as they can!

A piggyback ride keeps a **baby chimp** safe from harm.

Young chimpanzees enjoy playing in the trees. They grip the branches tightly with their hands and feet.

A special stick is useful for digging up ants to eat.

DISK LINK

 Visit the chimpanzee to piece together an amazing animal jigsaw puzzle!

Keeping clean is easy. You let your mother pick the twigs out of your fur!

Chimpanzees **pull faces** to talk to each other. This face means 'hello'.

A chimpanzee walks on all fours, leaning on its **knuckles**.

It's a fact!

A chimpanzee makes its own bed! Each night, it climbs up a tree and lays down twigs and leaves where it sleeps.

 # Amazing birds

There are hundreds of amazing birds on the grasslands. Giant ostriches run along the ground and tiny, colourful weaverbirds fly from tree to tree. You may even spot a hungry vulture swooping through the sky.

A vulture spots a snack from far away with a pair of beady **eyes**!

Silky **feathers** cover a vulture's body and keep it warm and dry.

A hooked **beak** is for tearing up chunks of food.

Ostriches cannot fly, but they can run very fast on their long, skinny legs!

DISK LINK

Visit the ostrich to play snakes and ladders in the grasslands!

24

It's a fact!

An ostrich lays the strongest eggs in the world. If you jump up and down on one, it still won't crack!

To fly, a vulture stretches out its two huge **wings**.

On the ground, a vulture hops along on its scaly **feet**.

A weaverbird works hard to build his nest. He collects strips of grass and weaves them into a ball on a branch.

Roaming around

During the day, many wild animals are out and about. They roam across the grass looking for tasty food to eat.

Which noisy animals are swinging through the trees?

Words you know

Here are some words that you learned earlier. Say them out loud, then try to find the things in the picture.

tusk	trunk	tail
feathers	beak	wing

27

The most amazing weaverbird nest of all time

Weaverbird was exhausted. He'd just finished weaving the last piece of long grass into his round nest, high up in the branch of an old thorny tree.

'Wow!' thought Weaverbird. 'That's the most amazing nest I've ever woven in my life. I must ask all the animals to come and look at it at once, while it's still fresh and green.'

Weaverbird looked around him. Way up on the highest branch, Vulture was cleaning his wings.

'I'll invite Vulture down to have a look,' he thought.

"Hey, Vulture," he shrieked, "hop down here and have a look at the most amazing weaverbird nest of all time."

"I'm not moving a claw," squawked Vulture. "I can see your nest quite clearly from here. I've been watching you all morning, weaving away, in and out and up and down. I thought you were never going to stop your nonsense. Anyway, my nest is much stronger and much better than yours. You should come up and take a closer look, that's if your little wings can carry you this high!"

"Oh, I know very well what your nest looks like," Weaverbird twittered back.

"It's nothing but a huge pile of old sticks, dead grass and feathers. You don't know how to weave at all!"

But before Vulture could ruffle his feathers, Weaverbird did a loop the loop and flew off.

As usual, Mother Rhino and her little baby were standing nearby, munching on their favourite bush.

'I'll ask them,' thought Weaverbird.

"Hey, Mother Rhino," he chirped, "stop eating for a minute, will you, and look up over your horn? I've just finished weaving the most amazing weaverbird nest of all time."

Mother Rhino slowly lifted her huge, grey head and looked straight into Weaverbird's tiny eyes.

"My eyesight is not too good you know," she said, talking with her mouth full. "I'm afraid all I can see is a little green blur. So it's a good job you told me where your nest is, because I might have mistaken it for a big, fat, juicy leaf."

"You're no use to me," cried Weaverbird. "You're as blind as a bat."

But before Mother Rhino could blink, Weaverbird did a loop the loop and flew off.

29

'I know what I'll do,' thought Weaverbird. 'I'll fly to the forest at the edge of the grass and ask the chimpanzees. They're awfully clever. I've seen them digging tiny insects out of the ground with sticks. They must have really good eyesight if they can see things that are so small.'

When Weaverbird landed in the forest, he could hear the chimps chattering and crashing about in the trees.

"Hey, chimps," he shouted through the leaves, "I've made the most amazing weaverbird nest of all time and I'd like you all to come and see it."

"Why should we swing all the way over there?" they hooted. "We're not interested in one of those teeny weeny, grass ball nests that you spend all day weaving, in and out and up and down.

We have the biggest and the most comfortable nests in the entire world. We build them every night out of fresh leaves and twigs."

"Every night before you go to sleep?" laughed Weaverbird. "What a complete waste of time!"

But before they could pull a face, Weaverbird did a loop the loop and flew off.

On his way back to the old thorny tree, Weaverbird looked down and saw Cheetah snoozing in the long grass.

'He looks like he's had a good dinner,' thought Weaverbird. 'Perhaps that's put him in a good mood.'

Weaverbird swooped down to where Cheetah lay and hovered by his head.

"Hey, Cheetah," he whispered, "I've made the most amazing weaverbird nest of all time. Would you like to see it?"

Cheetah opened his eyes and yawned, flashing his long, sharp teeth.

"I'm not scared of you," piped up Weaverbird. "Catch me if you can!"

But before Cheetah could open his mouth, Weaverbird did a loop the loop and flew off.

Feeling rather thirsty after all his squawking, Weaverbird decided to stop for a drink at the waterhole. Just as he dipped in his beak, a big herd of zebras joined him at the water's edge.

'They'll know a thing or two about grass,' thought Weaverbird. 'They spend all day with their noses in it.'

"Well knock my spots off," he hissed angrily. "You must be joking. I can't be bothered with all that fiddly weavy stuff. This whole grassland is my nest. When I want to relax, all I have to do is lie down in the grass or climb up a tree. Nobody ever bothers me, except irritating little birds like you." Cheetah stretched and then yawned. "Most of the animals keep out of my way. I usually go looking for them – when I am HUNGRY."

"Hey, zebras," he spluttered, "you know all about grass. Would you like to come over and look at the most amazing weaverbird nest of all time?"

"Oh yes, we'd love that," they replied enthusiastically. "All we ever do is eat and drink. It would be such fun to do something different."

"Well, follow me!" yelled Weaverbird. So the zebras quickly trotted after him to the bottom of the old thorny tree.

"So where exactly is your nest?" snorted the zebras.

"Stretch your necks and open your eyes," said Weaverbird bossily, pointing above their heads. "Look up there!"

"Wow!" said one zebra.

"That really is the most amazing weaverbird nest of all time," said another.

"You couldn't have made that all by yourself," said a third. "You must have had some help!"

"No," said Weaverbird proudly, "I made it all by myself."

"Well, well, well, well, well," said the zebras, one after the other.

"We've seen a lot of grass in our time, but we've certainly never seen anything this amazing. All that lovely green grass woven together to make a beautiful bird's nest. You must be extremely clever."

Weaverbird was thrilled. "Thank you, thank you," he said, taking a bow and hanging upside down from his nest, trying to impress the zebras with his bird acrobatics.

'The zebras know a lot about grass, so, if they think that my nest is the most amazing weaverbird nest of all time, it must be true!' he thought.

And with one final bow, Weaverbird did a loop the loop and flew off to look for a friend to share his lovely little nest.

Puzzles and activities

Now try out these puzzles and activities! If you want to do them again, you can print out copies from your disk!

Why not colour us in, first!

Animal match

Say the word lion out loud. Which letter sound does it begin with? Draw a line to match the lion with its letter sound. Do the same for the other animals.

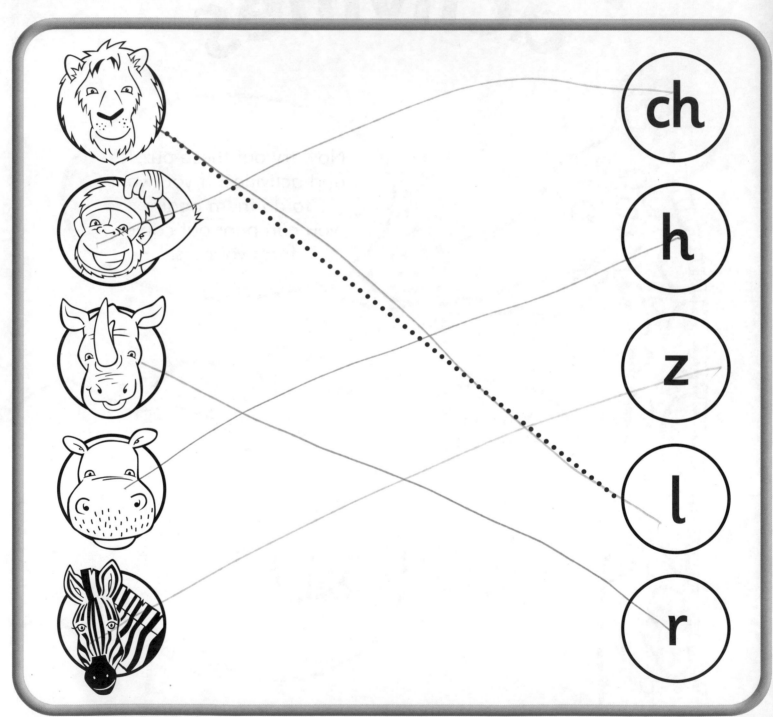

Animal antics

It's a hot day in the grasslands. Can you spot ten differences between these two pictures? When you find a difference, draw a ring around it on picture 2.

1

2

Name the animal

Can you match these wild animals to their names? Draw a line from the picture of the vulture to its name. Do the same for the other animals.

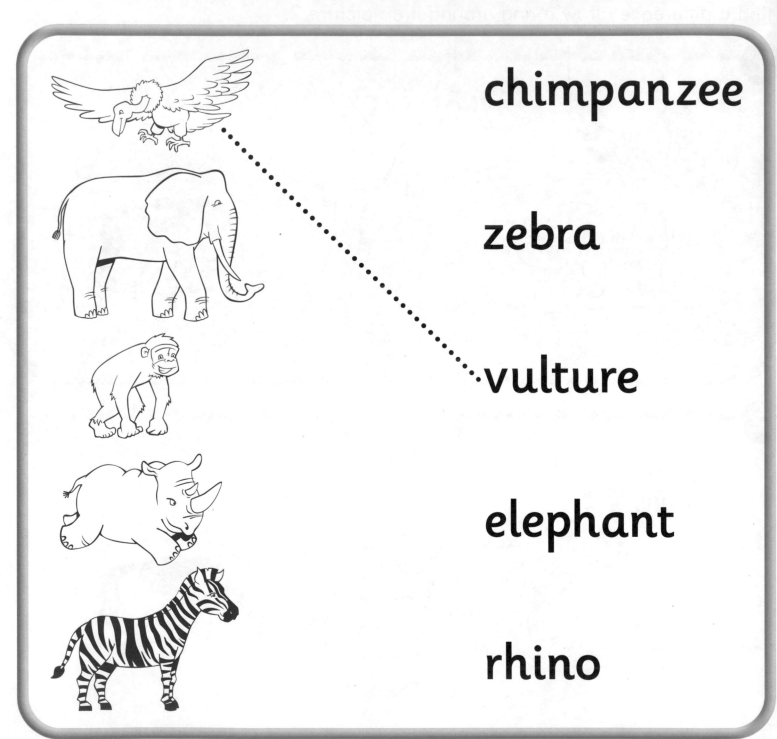

chimpanzee

zebra

vulture

elephant

rhino

Odd face out

Look at the row of rhinos. They are all exactly the same except for one. Circle the odd one out. Then do the same for the other rows.

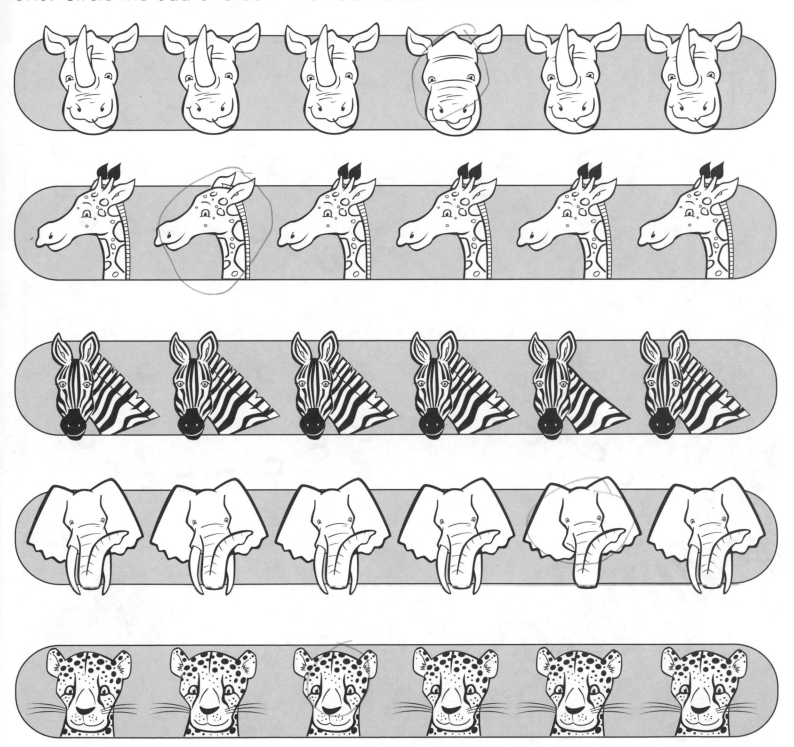

Track the animals!

Which animal is making which trail? Follow each set of footprints with your pencil to find out.

Capital match

Look at all the letters on this page. Draw a line to join the small **s** to the capital **S**. Now match the other small letters with their capital letters.

Missing words

Look at the zebra. Now match the words at the bottom of the page to the picture. Write each word in the right box. The first one is done for you.

tail

nose   stripes   tail   hoof

Now match the words to the elephant picture.

tusk   ear   trunk   leg

Creature features

Can you name these animals? Read the clues, then look at the animal names at the bottom of the page. Write your answer in each box.

Who am I?

I play in the trees.
I pull a face to say hello.
I scream loudly.

I'm a __ __ __ __ __ __ __ __ __ __ __ .

Who am I?

I have a spotty coat.
I can run very fast.
I have strong claws.

I'm a __ __ __ __ __ __ __ .

Who am I?

I have four legs.
My neck is very long.
I can reach tall trees.

I'm a __ __ __ __ __ __ __ .

cheetah   giraffe   chimpanzee

Animal quiz

Read the questions, then tick **Yes** or **No** to answer. You can find all the answers in this book! The first one is done for you.

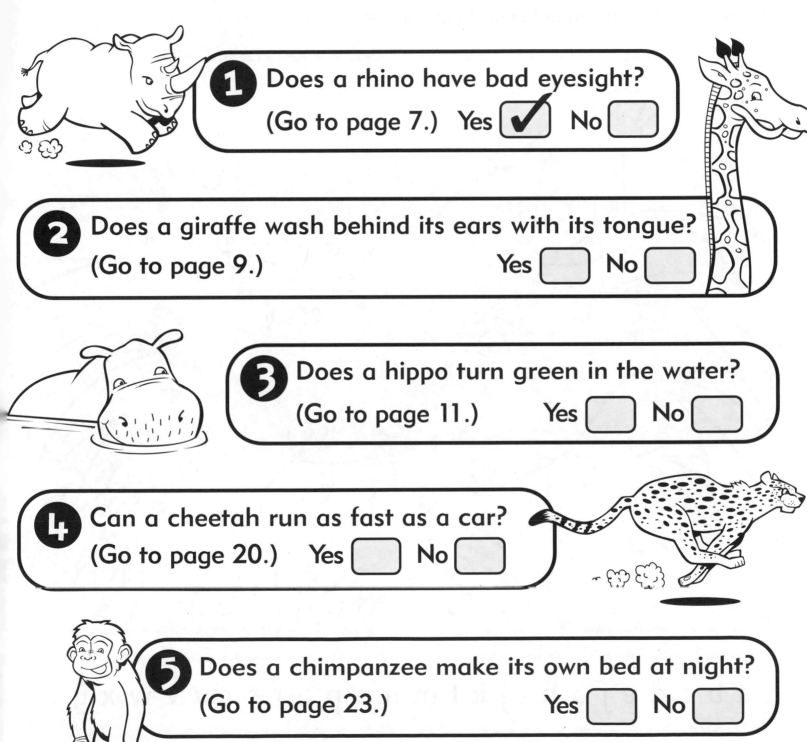

1 Does a rhino have bad eyesight?
(Go to page 7.)   Yes ✔   No ☐

2 Does a giraffe wash behind its ears with its tongue?
(Go to page 9.)   Yes ☐   No ☐

3 Does a hippo turn green in the water?
(Go to page 11.)   Yes ☐   No ☐

4 Can a cheetah run as fast as a car?
(Go to page 20.)   Yes ☐   No ☐

5 Does a chimpanzee make its own bed at night?
(Go to page 23.)   Yes ☐   No ☐

Dotty puzzle

What's in the picture? Find out by joining up the letters
in the order of the alphabet, starting from the letter **a**.
The alphabet is shown below to help you.

a b c d e f g h i j k l m n o p q r s t u v w x y z

Find the family

Draw a line through the maze to help the cheetah find its family. Then do the same for the other animals.

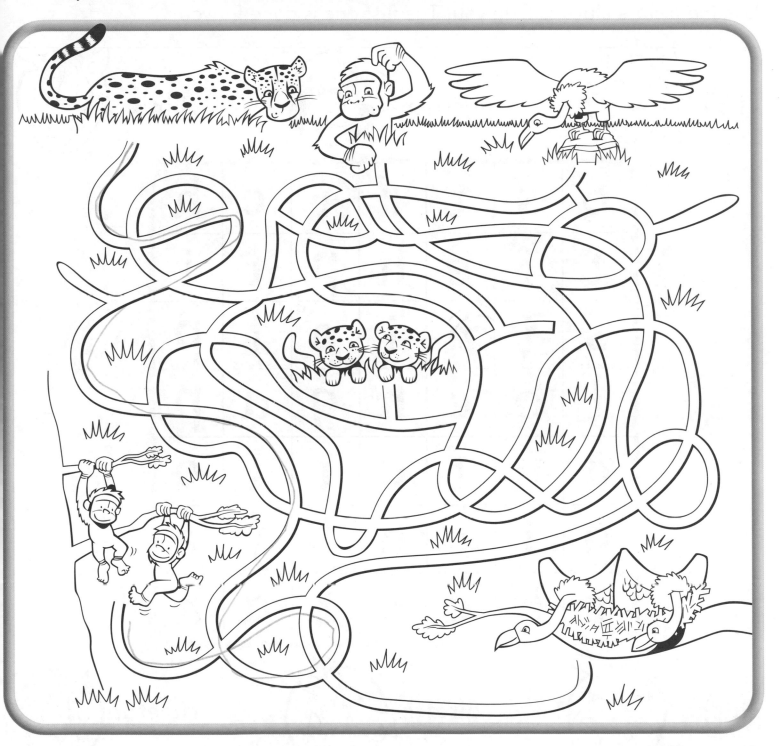

Wild wordsearch

There are six animal words hidden in the grid below. Can you find them? Look across from left to right or from top to bottom. Use the picture clues to help you. The first one is done for you.

lion

ostrich

rhino

o	s	t	r	i	c	h
t	l	e	h	p	l	i
s	i	h	i	o	f	p
l	o	e	n	g	a	p
a	n	t	o	i	l	o
g	i	r	a	f	f	e
c	h	e	e	t	a	h

hippo

giraffe

cheetah

46

Answers

page 34

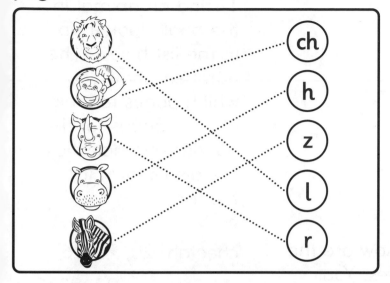

page 35

page 36

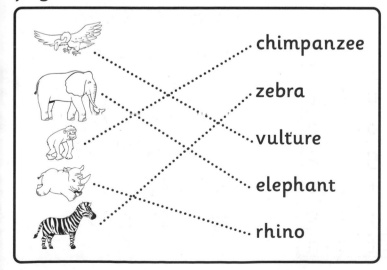

chimpanzee

zebra

vulture

elephant

rhino

page 37

page 37

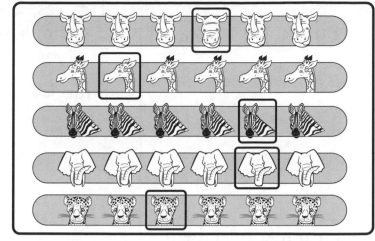

page 38

page 39

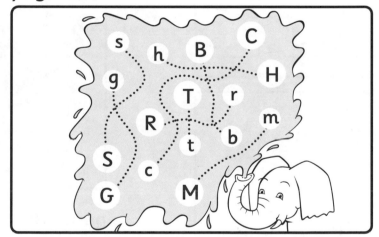

page 40

stripes

nose

tail

hoof

page 41

t u s k

e a r

t r u n k

l e g

page 42

I'm a chimpanzee.

I'm a giraffe.

I'm a cheetah.

page 43
1 = yes, 2 = yes,
3 = no, 4 = yes,
5 = yes.

page 44 rhino

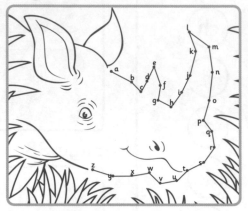

page 45 Below are the quickest routes. You may have found others.

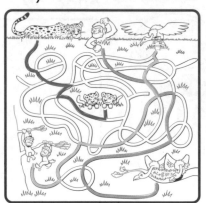

page 46

o	s	t	r	i	c	h
t	l	e	h	p	l	i
s	i	h	i	o	f	p
l	o	e	n	g	a	p
a	n	t	o	i	l	o
g	i	r	a	f	f	e
c	h	e	e	t	a	h

Index

To find an animal in the book, look it up in the list below. The numbers show you which pages to look at. The pages for the puzzles and activities are also shown in the list.